STILL

The World's Best Irish Jokes

In this series:

The World's Best Acting Jokes
The World's Best After-Dinner Jokes
The World's Best Boss Jokes
The World's Best Business Jokes
The World's Best Cricket Jokes
The World's Best Dirty Jokes
More of the World's Best Dirty Jokes
The World's Best Dirty Songs
The World's Best Doctor Jokes
The World's Best Drinking Jokes
More of the World's Best Drinking Jokes
The World's Best Fishing Jokes
The World's Best Football Jokes
The World's Best Gardening Jokes
The World's Best Golf Jokes
More of the World's Best Golf Jokes
The World's Best Holiday Jokes
The World's Best Irish Jokes
More of the World's Best Irish Jokes
Still More of the World's Best Irish Jokes
The World's Best Jewish Jokes
Still More of the World's Best Jewish Jokes
The World's Best Lawyer Jokes
The World's Best Light-bulb Jokes
The World's Best Marriage Jokes
The World's Best Mother-in-Law Jokes
The World's Best Motoring Jokes
The World's Best Scottish Jokes
The World's Best Skiing Jokes
The World's Best Sailing Jokes

STILL MORE OF The World's Best Irish Jokes

Des MacHale
Illustrated by Graham Morris

HarperCollinsPublishers

To Dominic –
The Last of our Little Jokes?

HarperCollins*Publishers*
77–85 Fulham Palace Road,
Hammersmith, London W6 8JB

This paperback edition 1995
1 3 5 7 9 8 6 4 2

First published in Great Britain by
Angus & Robertson (UK) 1990
Reprinted twice

Cover illustration by Tony Blundell

ISBN 0 00 638770 5

Set in Goudy

Printed in Great Britain by
HarperCollinsManufacturing Glasgow

INTRODUCTION

Well, all good things come to an end and this is definitely the last Irish joke book.

The astonishing success of my previous books shows that these jokes are an Irish art-form and not just insult and abuse as a few shallow people believe. Irishmen and Irishwomen have not been offended – they treat the jokes with a smile and a shrug of the shoulders as part of the price they must pay for greatness.

However, the joke has gone far enough and now the joke is over. Nothing short of an overdraft will persuade me to write another book of Irish jokes. But the need for humour and jokes continues in a world threatened by war, famine, pollution, unemployment, drugs and violence. What we desperately need is more laughter, because laughter eases pain and is the best and most effective medicine in the world, as well as being the cheapest. If you don't believe me, give a copy of this book to a friend who is ill or in hospital and see for yourself the rapid recovery. And there are no side effects except that the patient will be in stitches!

Why do Irishmen like swimming under water?
Because deep down they are quite intelligent.

An Irishman went on 'Mastermind' and chose as his special subject Irish history.

'In what year was the Easter Rising?' was his first question.

'Pass,' he replied.

'Who was the leader of the Easter Rising?'

'Pass,' he replied.

'Where did the Easter Rising take place?'

'Pass,' he replied.

'Good man, Seamus,' came a voice from the audience, 'tell them nothing.'

Why do Irish policemen have numbers?
In case they get lost.

Paddy was losing his hair so his friend suggested he get a transplant.

'No,' he replied, 'I'd look daft with a kidney on my head.'

The first people to invade the pitch were a party of Irishmen who ran in to the Coliseum to get the lions' autograph.

During a riot at an Irish prison, the Governor decided to call in the police to evict the troublemakers.

What is green and drives up the M1 in reverse?
An Irishman who knows the Highway Code backwards.

Why did the Irishman cross the road?
To get to the middle.

Seamus got a job with a big firm.

'Here,' said the boss, 'is a brush. Your first task is to sweep the floor.'

'Hold on,' said Seamus, 'I'm a university graduate.'

'OK,' said the boss, 'I'll show you how.'

Then there was the Irishman who applied for a half-price television licence because he had only one eye.

A rich man hired an Irishwoman to do his cleaning for him, but she failed to give satisfaction. Eventually he had to have a word with her but he tried to put it as gently as possible.

'You know Bridget,' he said to her one day, 'I can write my name on the dust on this desk.'

'Can you now sir?' she replied, 'isn't education a wonderful thing.'

A Kerryman asked a Dubliner how he was so smart. 'It's our diet,' said the Dubliner, 'and if you give me £50 I'll sell you some food that will make you smart too.'

'Done,' said the Kerryman, so the Dubliner sold him a pound of Dublin Bay prawns for £50 and the Kerryman ate them. When the Kerryman had bought the third batch of prawns for £50 he said to the Dubliner, 'Hold on a minute, I can buy those for £5 a pound in Moore Street.'

'Right,' said the Dubliner, 'just look how smart you're getting already.'

Have you heard about the Irishman who bought a farm in Alaska?

He wanted to grow frozen vegetables.

Where does Mick go on holiday?
To a different bar.

NOTICE IN AN IRISH NEWSPAPER: Manure for sale – fill it yourself £1 a bag.

Have you heard about the Cork nudist colony who bought a hundred blue ribbons and a hundred pink ribbons so they could tell the men from the women?

How do you recognise an Irish black magic session?
Everybody is eating hazelnut clusters.

Have you heard about the Irishman who used to walk into shops and leave things?
He was a maniokleptic.

Have you heard about the Irish cryptologist who has cracked the Highway Code?

How do you recognise an Irish football match?
The teams swap jerseys at half time.

Have you heard about the new Irish cookery series on TV?
It's called 'Pot Black'.

Have you heard about the Irishman who tried to commit suicide with an elastic rope?
He died of concussion.

A policeman knocked on an Irishman's door and told him a body had just been washed up on the beach and the authorities thought it might be his.

'What did he look like?' asked the Irishman.

'Well he was about your height and build,' said the policeman.

'And was he wearing serge trousers?' asked the Irishman, 'because I always wear serge trousers.'

'Actually he was,' said the policeman.

'What colour?' asked the Irishman.

'Blue,' said the policeman.

'That couldn't have been me,' said the Irishman, 'because I always wear black serge trousers.'

Have you heard about the Kerryman who failed his driving test?

His car rolled forward on a hill start.

What were the last words of the Irish gangster? Who put that fiddle in my violin case?

Lawyer: 'Do you wish to challenge any member of the jury?'

Paddy: 'I think I could fight that little fellow on the end.'

What happened to the Irish tadpole?
It turned into a butterfly.

Mick went into a hardware store and asked if he could buy a sink.

'Would you like one with a plug, sir?' asked the assistant.

'Don't tell me they've gone electric,' said Mick.

GULP
TWANG!

Have you heard about the Irish loan shark who lent out half a million pounds?

He immediately skipped town.

Quizmaster: 'Why are cows kept in a pasture?'
Murphy: 'So they will give pasteurised milk.'

Have you heard about the Irishman who lost all his teeth?

He slept with his head under the pillow and the fairies took them all during the night.

An Irishman walked into a bar and ordered nineteen pints of Guinness which he drank one after the other.

'Why do you have to drink so many pints?' a man at the bar asked him.

'See that sign over there?' said the Irishman, 'it says "nobody served under eighteen." '

Paddy: 'I think I need a pair of spectacles.'
Man in white coat: 'You certainly do – this is a fish and chip shop.'

Irish Preacher: 'Let us all get on our knees and thank God we are still on our feet.'

A court case was in session in Dublin where a German sailor had been charged with being drunk and disorderly.

'I cannot understand a word,' said the judge. 'Is there anybody in court who can translate what this man is saying?'

'I'm a fluent speaker of German,' said an Irishman, 'I'll do it.'

'Good,' said the judge, 'ask him what his name is.'

'Vot iss your name?' said the Irishman.

What is top of the bestseller list in Ireland this month?

'Memoirs of an Irish Kamikaze Pilot'.

An Irishman walked into a bar and asked the barman for a pint of less. 'Less?' said the barman, 'I'm not exactly sure if we stock that at the moment. Tell me what exactly is less?'

'I don't know,' said the Irishman, 'but the doctor told me I would have to drink less from now on.'

Paddy went to the optician's and the assistant asked him if his eyes had ever been checked.

'No,' said Paddy, 'they've always been blue.'

Quizmaster: 'Who was the first woman in the world?'

Seamus: 'I don't know.'

Quizmaster: 'I'll give you a clue – she had something to do with an apple.'

Seamus: 'Would it be Granny Smith?'

Have you heard about the Irishman who won a spot prize at a dance?

He had a total of 4,723 spots.

Murphy bought a fantastic new watch for £5 from a street trader. He was very proud of it because it was guaranteed waterproof, shockproof, anti-magnetic, with 237 jewels and accurate to within one millionth of a microsecond per light year. One night he was watching television with his wife when the 'News at Ten' came on the screen. Murphy looked at his watch and it said half-past eight. He screamed at his wife, 'Have you been messing about with that television set again?'

Paddy got a job on a submarine but got the sack after only a week. He insisted on sleeping with the windows open.

An Irishman complained to a friend at a dance that nobody would dance with him.

'Look,' said the friend, 'to be brutally honest with you, it's the smell from your socks. Go home, change them and when you come back to the dance you'll have girls falling all over you.'

An hour later they met again and the Irishman complained that there had been no improvement.

'Did you change your socks like I told you?' asked the friend.

'Of course I did,' said the Irishman producing the original pair from his pocket.

An Irish stunt driver decided to go for a world record by driving a bus off a ramp over a line of fifty motorbikes. He very nearly made it but halfway across someone rang the bell.

DING

Have you heard about the Irishman who had to take a pep-pill every morning to get enough energy to get out of bed so he could go to the chemists to buy his tranquillisers?

During the visit to this part of the solar system of Halley's comet, an Irishman was asked what he thought of this heavenly wonder. 'It's a sure sign of frost,' he replied.

Two Irishmen became terrorists and were driving around Belfast with a 200 pound bomb looking for a suitable place to plant it.

'Drive a bit more slowly,' said one to the other, 'or this blasted bomb will go off on my knees.'

'Don't worry,' said the driver, 'we've another one in the boot.'

Optician: 'Would you read the letters on this card please?'

Seamus: 'Would you mind reading it to me, because my sight isn't very good?'

Brendan was sending his young fellow down to the shop to buy some provisions.

'Get ten kilograms of spuds,' he told him, 'but don't get any big ones because they're too heavy to carry.'

An Irishman went to America where he became a policeman. One day he was assigned to keep order at a communist parade. Anxious to do his job well, the Irishman took his baton and hit an innocent spectator who was just looking at the parade.

'What did you do that for?' said the spectator, 'in fact I'm an anti-communist.'

'Look,' said the Irishman, 'I don't care what sort of communist you are.'

A very pious Irishman was hanging over a cliff by one arm so he prayed for God to save him. A boat passed by in the sea below and the boatman shouted for the Irishman to jump down and be rescued.

'No,' said the Irishman, 'God will save me.' A few minutes later a helicopter came dangling its rope ladder over the cliff and the pilot shouted out to the Irishman to grab the rope and be rescued.

'No,' said the Irishman, 'God will save me.' Finally a submarine surfaced and the captain called out to the Irishman to jump. 'No,' said the Irishman, 'God will save me.'

An hour later he fell off the cliff and was drowned. As he stood before God he said, 'God why didn't you save me?'

'Look,' said God, 'I sent a boat, a helicopter and a submarine, what more could I do?'

Paddy and Mick went to America and the first thing they saw when they landed was a hot dog stand.

'Will you look at that,' said Paddy. 'They eat dogs in this country.'

'They're very reasonable,' said Mick, 'we'll give them a try.'

So they bought two hot dogs and just as they began to eat, Paddy said to Mick, 'What part of the dog did you get?'

What happens to an Irishman who doesn't pay his garbage bill?

They stop delivering.

How do you recognise an Irish shoplifter?
He steals free samples.

Brendan was dancing with a girl at a ceili when she asked him if he knew the Walls of Limerick.

'Know them?' said Brendan. 'Wasn't my sister married to one of them?'

This fellow hired an Irishman to put in concealed lighting in his exclusive new house. The Irishman papered all over the switches.

Mick was out of work so he went around from house to house asking if there were any jobs to be done. One fellow felt sorry for him so he gave him a pot of yellow paint and a brush and told him to paint his porch yellow from top to bottom. About an hour later Mick, dripping in paint, came round for his money and said, 'The job is finished, oh, and by the way that's not a Porsche, it's a Mercedes.'

What did the Irishman say when the judge gave him 250 years in prison?

'If I hadn't had a smart lawyer I'd have got life.'

An old Dubliner was asked if he was in America during the Wall Street Crash.

'Of course I was,' he replied, 'didn't it nearly fall on top of me.'

Have you heard about the Irishman who was reading a book called *How to Bring up Children?*

One of his kids had just fallen down a well.

Paddy and his wife tried to make their sex life more exciting by making love in the bath. They had to give it up because they found the coal too lumpy.

Sean emigrated to England because he was told that the streets there were paved with gold and that all you had to do was to bend down and pick it up. As he got off the train in London on Saturday night he saw a five pound note lying on the platform so he bent down and picked it up. As he was just about to put it into his pocket he suddenly threw it away saying, 'I won't start until Monday.'

Have you heard about the Irishman who thought that a penal colony was an all-male, nudist camp?

Have you heard about the Irish electronics expert who has just invented the world's largest microchip?

Have you heard about the Irishman and his wife who were in the steel and iron business?
He did the stealing and she did the ironing.

An Irishman was missing for two weeks so his wife informed the police. One morning the police knocked on her door and told her that her husband's body had been found floating in the canal.

'Sure that couldn't be him,' she told them, 'because he couldn't swim.'

Paddy was complaining to a neighbour about the high cost of food.

'It's not like the old days,' he said to him, 'when you could make a meal out of nothing if you had the stuff.'

Two Irishmen were working on a building site and one day the first Irishman's wife arrived to see him while he was climbing up a ladder with half a ton of concrete blocks on his back.

'Don't turn round,' said the second Irishman, 'but look who's behind you.'

Have you heard about the Dubliner who crossed a dog with a tortoise?

It goes to the shop and brings back yesterday's newspaper.

What do you call an Irishman's boomerang that won't come back?

A stick.

Why did Seamus cross the road?

Because it was the chicken's day off.

Have you heard about the Irishman who invented the first telephone?

He had to wait twenty years for someone to invent the second telephone. Then when he rang him up found it was engaged.

Have you heard about the Irishman who went fly-fishing?

He caught a two-pound fly.

What does an Irish chiropodist have for his breakfast?

Corn flakes.

How many Irishmen does it take to change a lightbulb?

Two. One says to the other, 'Could you switch the light on in here Mick? It's so dark I can't see what I'm doing.'

Murphy was working on a building site and one day the foreman told him to go down a deep pit. Murphy stepped into the pit and fell thirty feet to the bottom.

'Why didn't you use the ladder?' shouted the foreman.

'I thought that was for coming up,' groaned Murphy.

Have you heard about the Irishman who thought that Chanel No. 5 was one of those new satellite television stations?

A sophisticated Kerryman was advising his younger brother who was just about to make a trip up the world's longest one way street – the road from Kerry to Dublin.

'Those fellows up in Dublin,' he told him, 'humour them, agree with them. Even if they say that Dublin is bigger than Killarney, agree with them.'

A Dubliner went to his doctor and told him that he had been feeling so depressed an hour previously that he had taken a hundred of the little yellow sleeping tablets that the doctor had prescribed for him the week before. Now he regretted his decision to commit suicide and asked the doctor to save him.

'Don't worry,' said the doctor, 'those were not sleeping tablets, they were laxatives.'

Mick and his wife were out one evening when burglars broke into their house. They called the police and reported all the things that were missing including jewellery and money.

'Was there any other damage, sir?' asked a policeman.

'No,' said Mick, 'but we had a pot of Irish stew cooking on the stove and one of them did something disgusting in it. We had to throw half of it away.'

A little Irish boy was doing his homework so he asked his father where the pyramids were.

'I don't know,' said his father, 'you should remember where you put things.'

Two Irishmen were escaping from jail so each of them hid up separate trees. As the police came by with tracker dogs to the first tree one of them shouted out, 'Who's up there?'

'Miaow, miaow,' went the first Irishman.

'Come away,' said the policeman, 'that's only a cat up there.'

They went to the second tree and the policeman shouted, 'Who's up there?'

'Another cat,' said the second Irishman.

What does a golfer get if he asks his Irish caddie for a sand wedge?

Corn beef in brown bread.

Have you heard about the Irishman who tried to commit suicide by taking a hundred aspirins?

After he took two he began to feel better.

Brendan went to a computer dating agency and he was fixed up with a girl who was a librarian.

On their first date he asked her, 'What part of Libraria are you from?'

Have you heard about the Irishman who stood outside a brothel for two hours waiting for the red light to turn green?

Mick went to the doctor and told him he had just swallowed a bone.

'Are you choking?' the doctor asked him.

'No,' said Mick, 'I'm serious.'

A Dubliner, a Corkman and a Kerryman each tendered for a big construction job in England, paid for by government money.

'I'll do it for £20,000,' said the Kerryman.

'How is that figure broken down?' asked the boss of the construction company.

'£10,000 for the materials and £10,000 for labour,' said the Kerryman.

'I'll do it for £40,000,' said the Dubliner, 'that's £20,000 for the materials and £20,000 for labour.'

'Look,' said the Corkman, 'my tender is for £60,000. That £20,000 for you, £20,000 for me and we'll give the other £20,000 to the Kerryman to do the job.'

Judge: 'Have you got a competent lawyer to defend you?'

Irishman: 'No, I haven't, but don't worry about me your honour, because I've got a few good friends on the jury.'

Brendan and Murphy, a bit worse for drink, awoke in a room in which the blinds were drawn.

'Is it day or night?' asked Brendan.

'I'll go and have a look,' said Murphy so he went over to the window, lifted the blind and looked out. Then he walked back and lay on his bed.

'Well,' said Brendan, 'is it day or night?'

'I can't remember,' said Murphy.

How do you get rid of an Irishman's car? Cover it with rust remover.

Paddy called into his bank and told the manager that he had just lost his new cheque book.

'Don't worry though,' he assured the manager. 'They won't be of any use to anybody who finds them because I've signed them all.'

Vet: 'Give your cow a tablespoon of this medicine three times a day.'

Irishman: 'I can't because the cow doesn't use a tablespoon. She drinks from a bucket.'

A Kerryman met a Dubliner who was carrying two large suitcases.

'Let me tell you about this fantastic new watch I've got,' said the Dubliner. 'It's accurate to a millionth of a microsecond and will tell you the time in Tokyo, San Francisco and Melbourne. It's got a built-in calendar, a calculator and a computer. It can tell you the date of any historical event, the time of the tide in any port of the world and the position of the planets at any time in the next thousand years.

'That's terrific,' said the Kerryman, 'tell me, what's in the suitcases?'

'That's the batteries,' said the Dubliner.

Have you heard about the new game that is all the rage in Kerry?

Two Kerrymen go into a darkened room together and then one of them leaves the room. The other one then tries to guess who left.

Two Irishmen went into an employment agency looking for jobs.

'What can you do?' the first was asked.

'I'm a fully qualified pilot,' said the first.

'Good,' he was told, 'we have vacancies for pilots at the moment.'

'How about you?' the second was asked.

'I'm a woodcutter,' said the second, 'one of the best in the business.'

'Sorry,' was the reply, 'we have no vacancies for woodcutters at the moment.'

'But,' said the second, 'how can he pile it if there's no one to cut it first?'

Seamus was asked in an interview what he thought of the American space programme.

'I don't know,' he replied, 'I never watch it.'

How does an Irishman keep flies out of his kitchen? He dumps a load of horse manure in his living room.

IRISH KNOCK-KNOCK:
Knock knock,
Who's there?
Michael Jackson,
Michael Jackson who?
Frank Sinatra.

The following small ad is said to have appeared in an Irish newspaper:

FOR SALE: A pair of wellingtons. Worn only once – from 1973 to 1984.

Paddy was asked by a census taker if he had any running water in his house.

'We used to have,' he replied, 'but we had the roof fixed a few years ago.'

Have you heard about the Irishwoman who moved from Dublin to Galway?

She wanted to be nearer her son in America.

Mick and his wife set up home in an old railway carriage parked in a siding on a closed branch-line. Mick got lots of exercise pushing the carriage up and down the track every time his wife went to the toilet.

At what Olympic events have Irishmen won medals?

Heading the shot and catching the javelin.

GOLD

An Irishman took his best suit in to be dry-cleaned. As he was to collect it he happened to notice that there was a large soup stain on the front. When he pointed this out to the assistant she said to him, 'You can't hold us responsible for that. It was there when you brought it in!'

Brendan went to the doctor and told him that he got a terrible pain in his arm every time he raised it over his head.

'Don't raise it over your head then,' said the doctor.

Two Irishmen were made redundant so they decided to use their redundancy money to set themselves up as painters. The local parish priest asked them to paint the church for him and they offered to do it for £1,000. However, paint proved to be a lot more expensive than they had envisaged and they found their stocks running out before they were even half finished. In desperation they bought gallons of turpentine and added it to their remaining paint and finished the job.

About a month later they called into the church to see how it looked and found large areas of paint peeling from the walls. As they sneaked out of the church they heard a booming voice calling out from above – 'Repaint you thinners.'

Have you heard about the Irishman who thought that *Ivanhoe* was a Russian gardener?

Denis O'Leary was an undertaker and one day a wealthy young woman came into his premises and identified a corpse as her father.

She gave orders for an expensive and elaborate funeral. Just as she was about to leave, the corpse's lower jaw opened and exposed a set of false teeth.

'My father didn't have false teeth,' she then shrieked, 'cancel that order.' Denis took the body out of the expensive coffin and said to it: 'You fool, you'd have had a first class funeral if only you'd kept your damn mouth shut.'

Two Irish businessmen met at Killarney railway station.

'Where are you going?' asked the first.

'Dublin,' said the second.

'You're telling me you're going to Dublin so I'll think you're going to Cork. But I happen to know from another source that you are going to Dublin, so there's no point telling me lies.'

A Kerryman's neighbour called to borrow his donkey but the Kerryman told him it was already lent. Just then the donkey brayed loud and clear in his stable.

'But you said your donkey was already lent,' protested the neighbour.

'He is,' said the Kerryman. 'Now who are you going to believe – the donkey or me?'

Bridget was called up for jury duty and was asked by the judge if she believed in capital punishment.

'I do,' said Bridget, 'if it's not too severe.'

Paddy went into a pet shop and told the assistant that he wanted a new mirror for his pet budgie.

'Would you like a large one or a small one sir?' asked the assistant.

'I don't rightly know,' said Paddy.

'Why not bring him into the shop sir?' said the assistant, 'and we'll try him out in front of a few mirrors and see which one he likes best.'

'That would never do,' said Paddy, 'it's for his birthday and I want it to be a surprise.'

First Irishman: 'The trouble with Englishmen is that they have no backbone.'

Second Irishman: 'They have backbone all right if only they would bring it to the front.'

First Irishman: 'What do you think of Englishmen?'

Second Irishman: 'Between you and me, some of them aren't the full fifty per cent.'

KITCHEN
MENU

English Foreman: 'I can lick any Irishman working for me.'

Brawny Irishman: 'You can't lick me and I'm an Irishman that's working for you.'

English Foreman: 'You're fired.'

An Irishman was up before the court charged with having his dog driving his car.

'Do you have anything to say in your defence?' asked the judge.

'Nothing,' said the Irishman, 'except that I once saw a horse talking on television.'

Have you heard about the Irishman who opened a restaurant where people could eat dirt cheap?

It went bust, because people didn't want to eat dirt.

Seamus went to the doctor suffering from some ailment so the doctor prescribed some medicine and told him to take two teaspoonsful of it every night an hour after taking a bath. A few weeks later Seamus returned and told him that there was no improvement in his condition.

'Did you carry out my instructions exactly as I told you?' asked the doctor.

'Not exactly,' said Seamus, 'I never managed to drink more than half a bath of water.'

An Irishman was back home telling his friends in the pub how thousands of people had come to meet him at the airport when he returned to the country.

'I don't believe anyone would turn out to welcome you back to the country,' said the barman.

'There were thousands and thousands of them,' said the Irishman, 'and if you don't believe me ask Bob Geldof, he was on the same flight.

A Dubliner was travelling by train and the ticket collector asked him where he was getting off.

'Killarney,' said the Dubliner.

'That's impossible,' said the ticket collector, 'we don't stop at Killarney on Tuesdays.'

'Look,' said the Dubliner, 'it's very urgent, I must get off at Killarney today.'

'I cannot break the regulations sir,' said the ticket collector.

'Look,' said the Dubliner, 'it's really very urgent, here's £100, get the driver to slow down a bit and I'll jump off.'

So the ticket collector agreed while warning the Dubliner to keep running after his feet touched the platform or otherwise he would be badly injured.

As the train came into Killarney it slowed to a crawl and the Dubliner jumped off and ran furiously along the platform. As he neared the front of the train a dining carriage attendant grabbed him and pulled him on board saying: 'You're very very lucky to have made it because we don't stop at Killarney on Tuesdays.'

Have you heard about the Irishman who got a job as a public toilet attendant?

They had to let him go because he couldn't remember the prices.

Paddy was charged with deserting his wife.

'I award your wife £500 a month,' said the judge.

'That's very generous of your honour,' said Paddy. 'I'll try and give her a few quid myself as well.'

Irish preacher at a funeral service: 'My dear brothers and sisters, this corpse was a member of our congregation for the last twenty-five years.'

Once there was a serious earthquake in Kerry. It did ten million pounds worth of improvements.

An Irishman was about to be hung for murder when a telegram arrived. The executioner opened the telegram and began to laugh out loud.

'Have I been given a last minute pardon?' asked the Irishman anxiously.

'No,' laughed the executioner, 'but you've just won £250,000 in the National Lottery.'

A tourist arrived at an Irish hotel. The porter took his bags and said to him, 'Follow me sir, I'll be right behind you.'

Two Irishmen were out driving together.

'Are we getting near a town?' asked the first.

'We must be,' said the second, 'because we seem to be knocking down more people.'

'Well drive slower then,' said the first.

'What do you mean, drive slower?' said the second. 'You're driving aren't you?'

Have you heard about the Irishman who opened a topless restaurant.

It had no roof.

Why don't Irishmen eat Smarties?

It's too much trouble peeling off the shells to get to the chocolate.

During a flight from Dublin to London a businessman in the non-smoking section of the aircraft suddenly felt the need for a smoke. As there were several vacant seats in the smoking area he asked the hostess if he could change seats. She allowed him to do so and he found himself seated next to a talkative Irishman.

'It's nice to meet you,' said the Irishman, 'did you get on just now.'

TOPLESS
RESTAURANT

Corkman: 'Do you spend all day going up that ladder?'

Kerryman: 'No, half the time I come down.'

An Irishman applied for a job as a street cleaner and was told that he would have to take an intelligence test.

'What does psychocybernetics mean?' asked the examiner.

'It means,' said the Irishman, 'that I'm not going to get the job.'

Paddy had lost an arm but always kept his wristwatch on the stump of the arm he had lost.

'Wouldn't it be more convenient to keep it on the good arm?' a friend asked.

'And what would I wind it with?' said Paddy.

An Irishman went into a shop and asked for a bottle of sauce.

'Certainly sir,' said the girl behind the counter, 'would you like HP?'

'No,' said the Irishman, 'I'm paying cash.'

'How is business?' a Dublin trader was asked.

'Terrific,' he replied, 'I bought a tractor for £10,000, traded it for two cars, traded each of them for two motor bikes, traded each of the motor bikes for four racing bicycles and finally sold the racing bicycles for £10,000.'

'But you didn't make a profit.'

'Maybe not,' said the Dubliner, 'but look at all the business I did.'

What is the happiest five year period of an Irishman's life?

Junior infants.

What do you do to a one-armed Irishman hanging from a tree?

Wave to him.

Doctor: 'You have been very badly injured in an accident. Please tell me your name so I can inform your wife.'

Seamus: 'There's no need to. My wife already knows my name.'

Paddy went to his doctor and asked him to give him something for the wind.

The doctor gave him a kite.

Have you heard about the Irishman who was caught stealing the lead off the roof of Fort Knox?

Mick was boasting about his son, 'He's one of the cleverest lads in the country,' he told a friend, 'he's always helping the police with their enquiries.'

Seamus went into a posh restaurant with his wife and ordered an expensive bottle of wine.

'Certainly, sir,' said the waiter, 'which year?'

'I'll have it right away,' said Seamus, 'if you don't mind!'

Paddy went into hospital for an operation and woke up shouting, 'Doctor, Doctor, I can't feel my legs!'

'I know,' said the doctor, 'I've just cut your arms off!'

An Irishman broke into a gambling casino in Las Vegas. When the police caught him he was $3,000 down.

This fellow went into a pub and seated at the bar was an Irishman with the biggest dog he had ever seen.

'Does your dog bite sir?' he asked the Irishman.

'No,' said the Irishman, 'my dog is as gentle as a lamb.'

So the fellow went over and patted the dog and the dog nearly bit his arm off.

'I thought you told me your dog didn't bite,' he screamed at the Irishman.

'That's right,' said the Irishman, 'but that's not my dog.'

Have you heard about the Irish acid bath murderer? He lost an arm taking the stopper out of the plughole.

A newspaper once published the following retraction of an Irish news item:

Instead of being jailed for murdering his wife by pushing her downstairs and throwing a lit oil lamp after her as we reported last week, we believe that the Reverend Roger MacIntosh in fact died unmarried four years ago.

Brendan and Seamus were waiting as a bus came along.

'Is this a one-man bus?' Brendan asked the driver.

'It is,' replied the driver.

'We'll wait for the next one,' said Seamus, 'because we both want to get on!'

Why does an Irishman's car have heated rear windows?

To keep his hands warm while he is pushing it!

Why was the Irishman jumping up and down on a hedgehog?
He wanted a big chestnut.

Have you heard about the Irishman who burned himself severely at a Halloween party?
He was bobbing for chips.

Why do Irish businessmen not take coffee after lunch?
It keeps them awake all afternoon.

Have you heard about the Irishman who was a trade union dentist?
His motto was 'one out – all out'.

$500
CIGARS

Mick got a job as a zoo keeper to one of the world's rarest female gorillas. The gorilla, however, had refused to mate with all the male gorillas that the zoo authorities had flown in from abroad at great expense. In desperation they asked Mick if he would mate with the gorilla for £5,000. He agreed on three conditions:

(i) That the gorilla be given a thorough bath.

(ii) That any offspring resulting from the union would be raised as Irish Catholics.

(iii) That he be given a month to raise the £5,000.

A Kerryman was the oldest man in Ireland and had reached the remarkable age of a hundred and twenty years. A national newspaper sent their top reporter to interview him on the occasion of his birthday.

'To what do you attribute your great age?' the reporter asked him.

'To the fact that it is so long since I was born,' said the Kerryman with a twinkle in his eye.

'Let us be serious,' said the reporter, 'why have you

lived to a hundred and twenty?'

'Vitamin pills,' said the Kerryman, 'I've been taking a vitamin pill every day since I was a hundred and ten!'

Paddy went to the doctor and told him that he needed some medical attention.

'What seems to be the problem?' asked the doctor.

'Well doc,' said Paddy, 'it's just that I go to the toilet regularly at seven o'clock every morning.'

'That's splendid,' said the doctor, 'why should you be worried about that?'

'I don't get up until eight o'clock,' said Paddy.

First Irishman: 'The clock goes back this week.'

Second Irishman: 'You should have kept up with the repayments.'

Have you heard about the Irish nightclub that employed a chucker-in?

Have you heard about the Irishman who died in China?

They buried him in a paddy-field.

What does an Irishman say while making an obscene telephone call?

'Stop telling me the time while I'm talking to you.'

Seamus went to the dentist and asked him to take all his teeth out.

'All of them?' said the dentist.

'Yes,' said Seamus, 'all of them.'

So the dentist took out all his teeth.

'April fool!' said Seamus. 'All I have is a sore finger.'

Afterwards a friend asked him what it was like having all his teeth out.

'Never again,' said Seamus, 'never again.'

Have you heard about the Irishman who had six O levels?

He had O in mathematics, O in science, O in geography, O in history, O in Latin and O in French.

Mick applied for a job as head book-keeper with a big firm and was being interviewed by the top directors of the company.

'So you would like to become our head book-keeper, would you?' asked one director.

'That's right,' said Mick, 'I would indeed.'

'And tell me,' said the director, 'what experience have you?'

'A lot of experience,' said Mick, 'I have two library books that have been overdue for over six months.'

This fellow went into a garage owned by an Irishman and asked him to check the tyres.

The Irishman walked round the car, kicked each of the tyres in turn and said to him:

'You're fine, you have four of them.'

Have you heard about the Irishman who tunnelled his way to freedom from prison in two months?

He was only serving one month.

Paddy went to a psychiatrist and told him he was having some problems.

'Describe your symptoms to me,' said the psychiatrist.

'Sometimes I feel I'm a wigwam,' said Paddy, 'and sometimes I feel I'm a teepee.'

'You're too tense,' said the psychiatrist.

NEWS ITEM: Late last night an Irishman fell into an upholstery machine. Latest reports say he is now fully recovered.

Seamus was before the court charged with driving his car at over a hundred miles an hour.

'What is your excuse?' asked the judge.

'Look, your warship,' said Seamus, 'I do everything very quickly.'

'Let's see how quickly you can do fourteen days,' said the judge.

Murphy was being interviewed for the post of chief accountant and financial officer for a big company and he made a big impression on the board of directors.

'Well,' said the chairman of the board, 'we have decided to appoint you to the position at an annual salary of £38,000.'

'That's great,' said Murphy, 'how much a week does that work out at?

An Irishman went into a hardware shop and asked the assistant if he had long nails.

'Certainly, sir,' said the assistant, 'how long do you want them?'

'I want to keep them,' said the Irishman.

Paddy and Mick were drinking late one night and found themselves stranded in town at midnight without even a taxi fare.

'I'll tell you what,' said Paddy, 'let's break into the bus garage and steal a number 10.'

'Right,' said Mick.

After about half-an-hour of the most ferocious banging and crashing he emerged with a number 10 explaining that the number 10s were all at the back.

'Couldn't you have taken a number 14 and we could have got off at the supermarket,' hissed Paddy. 'Now I'll go down to the bus stop and you pick me up there.'

But Mick whizzed past the bus stop and when Paddy arrived home an hour later wet and exhausted he explained, 'It was a request stop and you didn't put your hand out.'

Have you heard about the Irishman who wouldn't buy a Japanese transistor radio because he wouldn't be able to understand what they were saying?

An Irish plumber was on a world tour and on the second week of the tour he was being shown around North America. The highlight of the visit was a trip to Niagara Falls.

'What do you think of that?' asked the guide, waiting for the amazed reaction.

'If I hadn't left my bag of tools at home,' said the Irishman, 'I could fix the leak that's causing that.'

A bit taken aback, the guide continued, 'I'll have you know that a billion gallons of water fall over the edge every day.'

'Sure why wouldn't it?' said the Irishman, 'what's to hinder it?'

Seamus went to the doctor and told him he was having some digestive trouble.

'What have you been eating?' asked the doctor.

'Snooker balls,' said Seamus.

'How many do you eat every day?'

'About a dozen,' said Seamus. 'I have three reds for breakfast, a blue and a black for lunch followed by a

MICKS
PLUMBING
NIAGARA
FALLS

brown and a blue, four reds for dinner, and a yellow and a pink for tea.'

'That's your trouble,' said the doctor. 'You're not eating any greens.'

Have you heard about the Irishman who got a terrific job as a taxi-driver?

He gave it up because he couldn't stand people talking behind his back.

Mick rang the police and asked them if they could come and help him.

'What's the trouble sir?' asked the policeman.

'I've locked my keys in the car,' said Mick.

'We'll be round right away, sir,' said the policeman.

'Please hurry,' said Mick, 'it's pouring with rain and I've left the sun-roof open.'

An Irishman walked into a clothing store and asked to see the cheapest suit in the shop.

'You're wearing it sir,' said the assistant.

What do you give an eighty-year-old Irishman who marries an eighteen-year-old girl?

Jump leads.

Have you heard about the Irishman who had to give up his job as a fireman?

It used to take him nearly two hours to slide back up the pole.

Brendan received an emergency phone call at work that his house had been blown away in a hurricane.

'It couldn't have,' said Brendan, 'I have the key right here in my pocket.'

Liam was having problems with his weight so his doctor advised him to do some jogging.

'How much should I jog?' Liam asked.

'About ten miles a day,' said the doctor, 'and ring me in a week.' After a week Liam rang to say he was getting on fine with his jogging but that he was seventy miles from home.

Why do Irishmen wear bowler hats?
To protect their heads from woodpeckers.

Sean and Mick were complaining about how lazy their sons were.

'Look at my fellow,' said Sean, 'he's so lazy he just sits looking at the television all day.'

'So does my fellow,' said Mick, 'but he's too lazy even to switch it on.'

An Irishman joined the army and was being interviewed by an officer to see what regiment he was suitable for.

'Can you fire a gun?' asked the officer.

'No,' said the Irishman.

'What can you do?' asked the officer.

'I can take messages, sir,' said the Irishman.

'Good,' said the officer, 'I think we will assign you to the pigeon corps in charge of vital messages being carried from the front by pigeons.'

The Irishman underwent a week's intensive training in the pigeon corps and on his first morning on the job a pigeon arrived from the front bearing a message.

'Quick,' said the officer, 'go and see what the message is.'

About an hour the Irishman returned, bleeding and torn and covered in feathers and pigeon droppings.

'Well,' said the officer, 'what was the message?'

'Coo, coo,' said the Irishman.

An Englishman, a Scotsman and an Irishman were stranded on a little island in the middle of the Pacific Ocean and one day they found a magic bottle. When they rubbed it, a genie appeared and granted them each any one wish they desired.

'I'd like to be back in London,' said the Englishman and he was whisked away.

'I'd like to be back in Glasgow,' said the Scotsman and he too was whisked away.

'I'm very lonely here all on my own,' said the Irishman, 'I wish my friends were back again.'

An Irishman claimed that Ireland must be the healthiest country in the world.

'Why else,' he asked, 'would the government be closing all the hospitals?'

Why do Irishmen carry umbrellas when it's not raining?

Because umbrellas can't walk.

Seamus got a part in a play where he had only one line to say – 'Hark, I hear a pistol shot!'

He went around for months beforehand practising his line and driving everybody mad saying: 'Hark, I hear a pistol shot!'

On the opening night of the play he came on stage and when the gun went off he shouted: 'What the hell was that noise?'

How do you recognise an Irishman's word processor? The screen is covered in Tippex.

Paddy was before the court charged with riding a bicycle with no light on.

'How do you plead?' the judge asked him.

'Guilty, your honour,' said Paddy, 'but insane.'

Policeman to the Irishman: 'What's your name?'

Irishman: 'Happy birthday to you, happy birthday to you, happy birthday dear Mick – it's Mick.'

Brendan: 'I was reading in a book the other day that we use only a third of our brains.'

Murphy: 'What do we do with the other third?'

Two Irishmen were out flying when their plane caught fire. The first Irishman bailed out and pulled the cord of his parachute which opened immediately. The second Irishman jumped out, pulled the cord, but nothing happened. He went zooming towards the ground at high speed. The first Irishman pulled a knife from his pocket as he saw him pass and began to cut at his parachute straps shouting: 'Sure if you want a race I'll give you one.'

The general manager of a large banking group was travelling around the country incognito checking up on the efficiency of his branches. He came to a little branch in Kerry where the bank was closed during banking hours and the three clerks were playing poker behind the counter with the bank's money. To give them a fright, he rang the alarm bell three times but none of them moved. However, a few minutes later the barman from the pub across the road brought over three pints of stout.

Sign seen on a road in Cork:
TO MAKE A RIGHT TURN
MAKE THREE LEFT TURNS.

An Irishman was taking an intelligence test. 'What is black,' asked the examiner, 'and is worn on the foot in wet weather?'

'I don't know,' said the Irishman.

'It's a wellington boot,' said the examiner. 'Now think before you answer the next question. "What are black and worn on the feet in wet weather?" '

'I don't know,' said the Irishman.

'It's a pair of wellington boots,' said the examiner. 'Now think before you answer the final question. "Who lives in the White House and rules over millions of Americans?" '

'I know that one,' shouted the Irishman thinking deeply. 'It's three wellington boots.'

Have you heard about the Irish village that was too small to have a village idiot so they all took turns?

This little fellow parked his car in a narrow little laneway near an Irishman's house, so the Irishman came out and asked him to shift it.

'Why should I?' said the fellow, 'After all it's a cul-de-sac, isn't it?'

'Look,' said the Irishman, 'I don't care what make it is, shift it.'

Have you heard about the Belfast surgeon?

He had just performed the world's first hernia transplant.

There was an Irishman in a bar who ordered twenty-seven half-pints of stout and drank them down one after the other.

'Why don't you drink pints instead sir?' asked the barman, 'it would be a lot more convenient.'

'I used to drink pints,' said the Irishman, 'but the doctor told me they were making me terribly fat, so now I drink half-pints instead.'

Paddy called round to see Mick and was astonished to find his friend's son hammering nails into the furniture.

'Why do you let him do that?' he asked.

'It keeps him out of mischief,' was the reply.

'Isn't it a bit expensive?' asked Paddy.

'No,' said Mick, 'not a bit. I get the nails free at work.'

This fellow was staying on an Irishman's farm and he couldn't help noticing that one of the pigs had a wooden leg. Naturally he asked the Irishman why.

'Well,' said the Irishman, 'that's quite a remarkable pig. One night when we were all asleep, the house caught fire. That pig roused the entire household and saved two of the children single-handed.

'A few weeks later he was out digging on the land

when he discovered oil that's bringing me in a small fortune and recently I've found out that he is working on a new language so that pigs can communicate with human beings.'

'But why the wooden leg?' said the fellow.

'You couldn't eat a pig like that all in one go,' said the Irishman.

Irishman to garage proprietor: 'Would you have a truncated, hexagonal gasket for a blue van?'

Paddy was suffering from BO so his girlfriend advised him to go home have a bath and afterwards use deodorant and toilet water. Next day she met him with his head all covered in bandages.

'What happened?' she asked him.

'The toilet seat hit me on the head,' said Paddy.

Two Irishmen were walking along a golf course when suddenly there was a shout of 'Fore' and a golf ball came flying through the air and hit one of them on the head.

'Watch out,' said the other Irishman throwing himself on the grass. 'There are three more to come!'

Have you heard about the Irishman who was so tall he had to climb a ladder to shave himself?

How many Irishmen does it take to make popcorn? Ten. One to hold the pan and nine to shake the cooker up and down.

Brendan had his car stolen by a man he thought was his friend and due to a technicality the fellow got off scot free.

'He'll regret it to his dying day,' said Brendan, 'if ever he lives that long.'

An Irishman went into the post office and asked for a licence for his dog.

'Certainly,' said the clerk, 'what's the name?'

'Fido,' said the Irishman.

How long does it take an Irishman to write a note to the milkman?

About an hour – even longer if he forgets to write on the paper before he puts it into the bottle.

Have you heard about the Irish cannibal who went on a self-catering holiday?

He came back with two wooden legs.

Paddy: 'What is that on your leg?'

Mick: 'A birthmark.'

Paddy: 'How long have you had it?'

How do you recognise an Irishman shaving with a electric razor?

He's got the bathroom covered in foam.

One of the world's richest men had a set of dominoes in which there were huge diamonds instead of spots. One night an Irishman broke into his house and stole the double blank.

'What have you got in your pocket?' one Irishman asked another.

'I'll give you a clue,' said the second, 'it begins with the letter N.'

'A napple,' said the first Irishman.

'No,' said the second, 'I told you it begins with the letter N.'

'A norange,' said the first Irishman.

'No, no,' said the second, 'I'm telling you for the last time that it begins with the letter N.'

'Would it be a nonion?' said the first Irishman.

'You got it at last,' said the second Irishman.

There's a fantastic new restaurant just opened in Cork. Inside the door there's a big tank of water. The waiter hands you a net and you can choose any steak you want.

Foreman: 'I thought you promised me that you would have that work finished this evening.'

Paddy: 'I'll have it done this evening even if it takes me until tomorrow night.'

NOTICE IN AN IRISH NEWSPAPER:
FOR SALE Twelve donkeys male and female reasonably priced to clear.

P.S. four of the above have already been sold.

How do you recognise an Irishman's dishwasher?
It's all clogged up with paper plates.

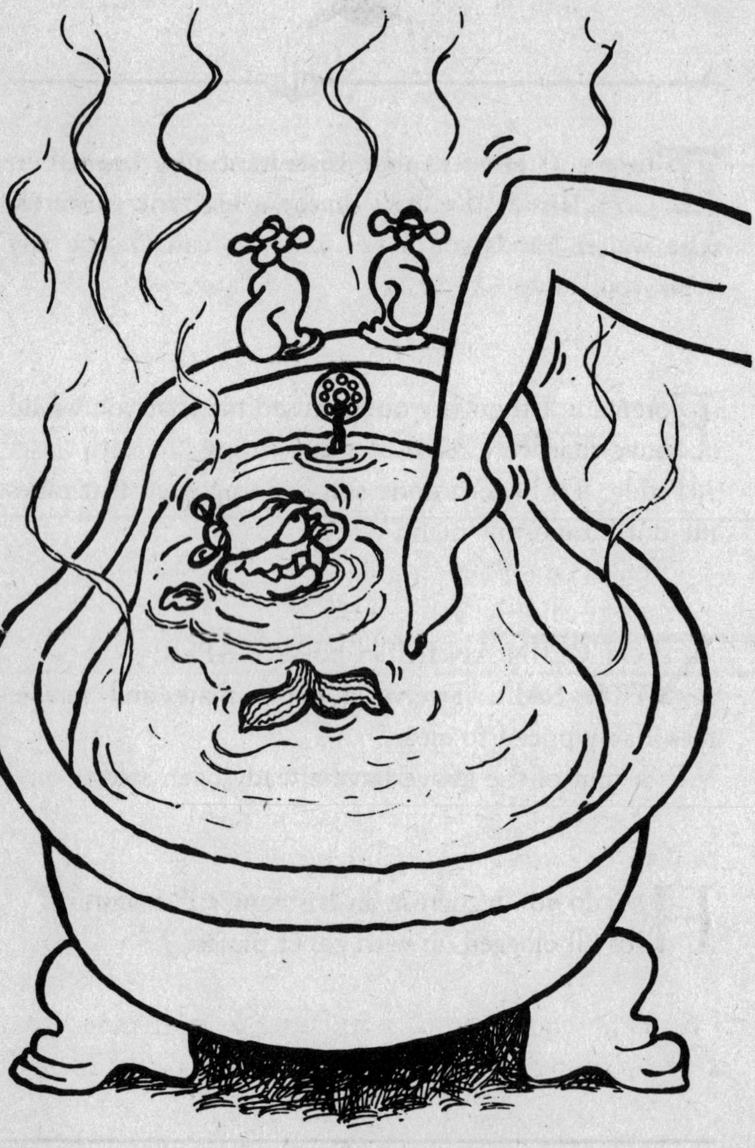

Bridget: 'I keep my goldfish in the bathtub.' Brendan: 'What do you do when you want to take a bath?'

Bridget: 'I blindfold it.'

Seamus went to New York and was driving round in a cab and the cab driver asked him the following riddle – Who has the same father and mother as me but is not my brother and not my sister?

'I don't know,' said Seamus.

'It's me,' said the cab driver.

'Begob,' said Seamus to himself, 'that's a good one.' So when he got home he tried it out on the lads in the pub.

'Who has the same parents as me but is not my brother and not my sister?' he asked them.

'We don't know,' they all replied.

'It's a cab driver in New York,' shouted Seamus.

A new young Irish horticultural instructor was appointed in Kent and was doing a tour of the

county. He found one old farmer in the orchard and began to lay down the law about his out-of-date methods of fruit growing.

'Look at this tree,' he said, 'it's not properly pruned, not properly fertilised and it's planted in the wrong place. I'd be surprised if you get ten pounds of apples off that tree.'

'So would I,' said the farmer, 'that's a pear tree.'